What's This Gadget For?

*a quizbook about kitchen tools found and enjoyed
in an old family summer place by the lake*

Shelly Errington

When I inherited my great aunt Matty's modest old summer place
on a beautiful lake, I found that nothing had ever been thrown away.
As a tribute to both nature and culture, I have created
a kind of visual quiz book combining images from both.

You'll find answers at the end.

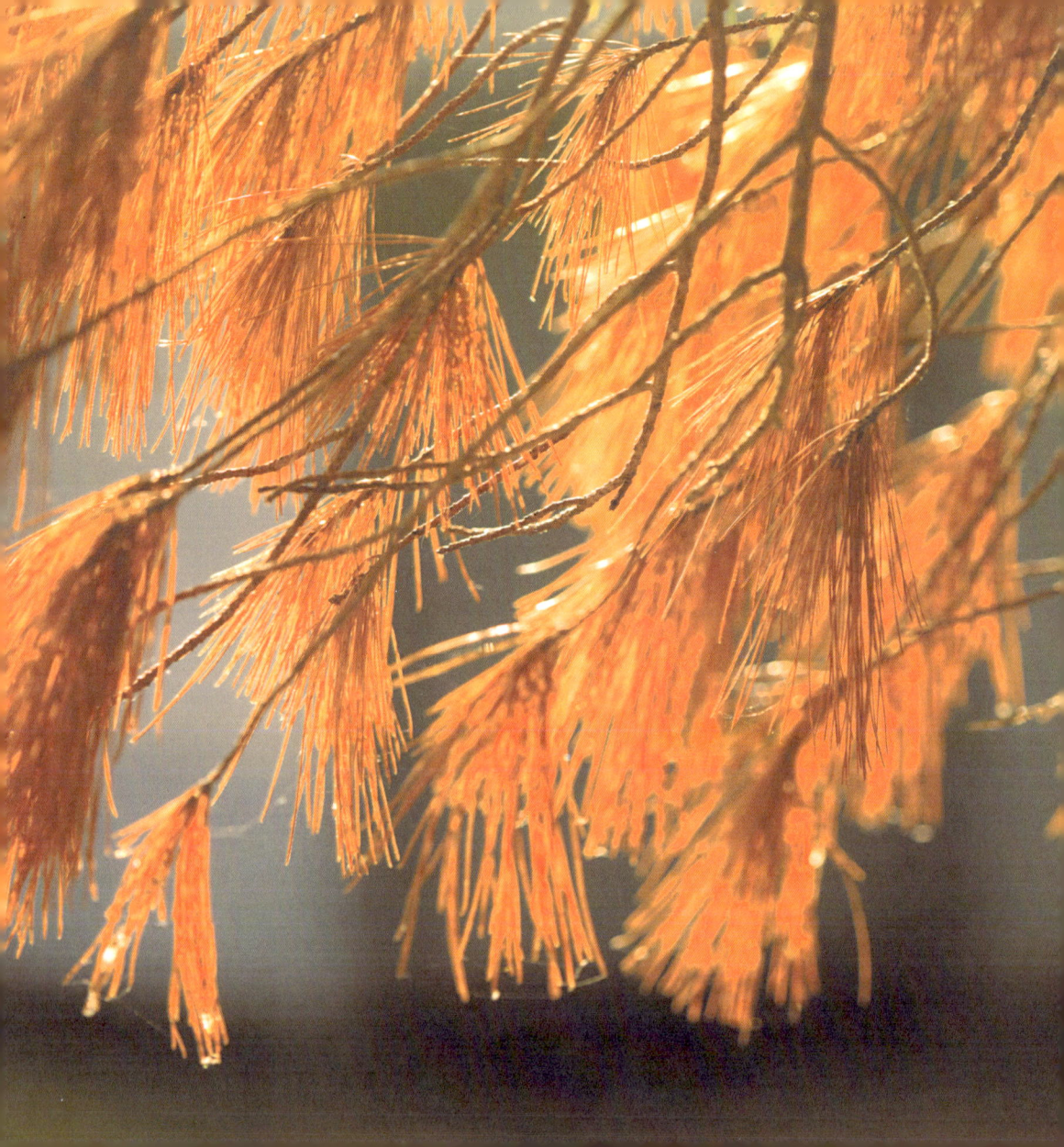

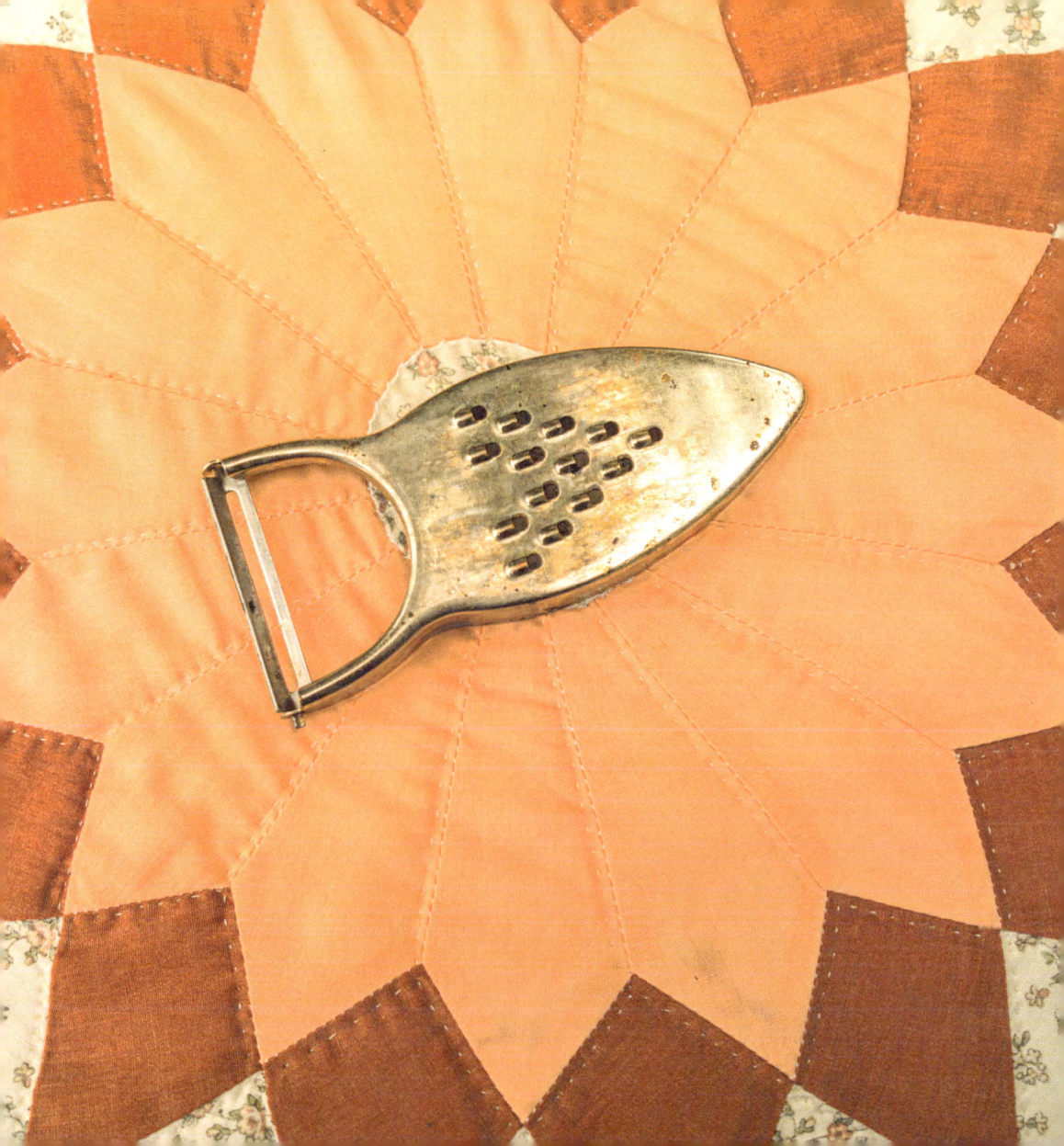

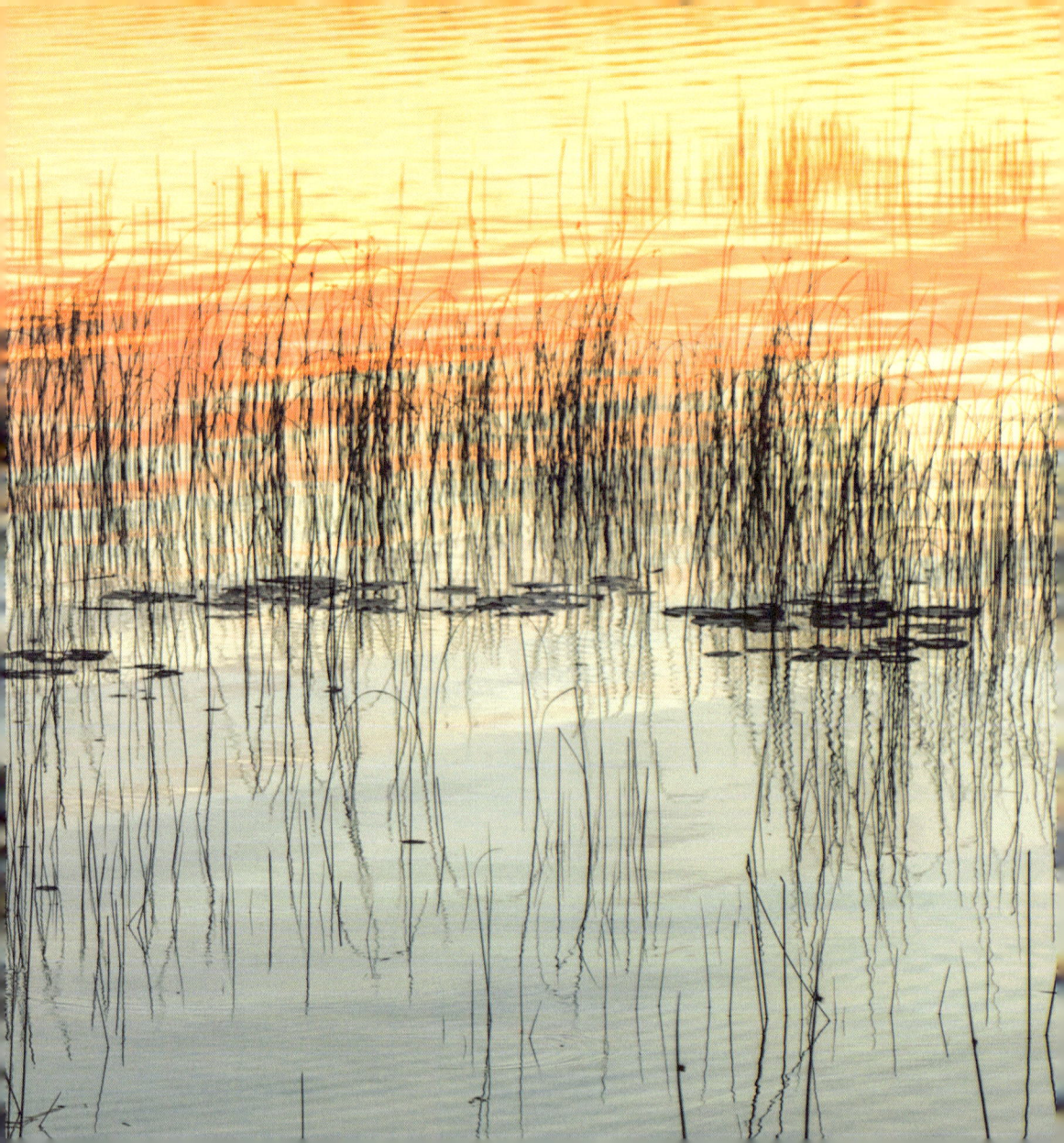

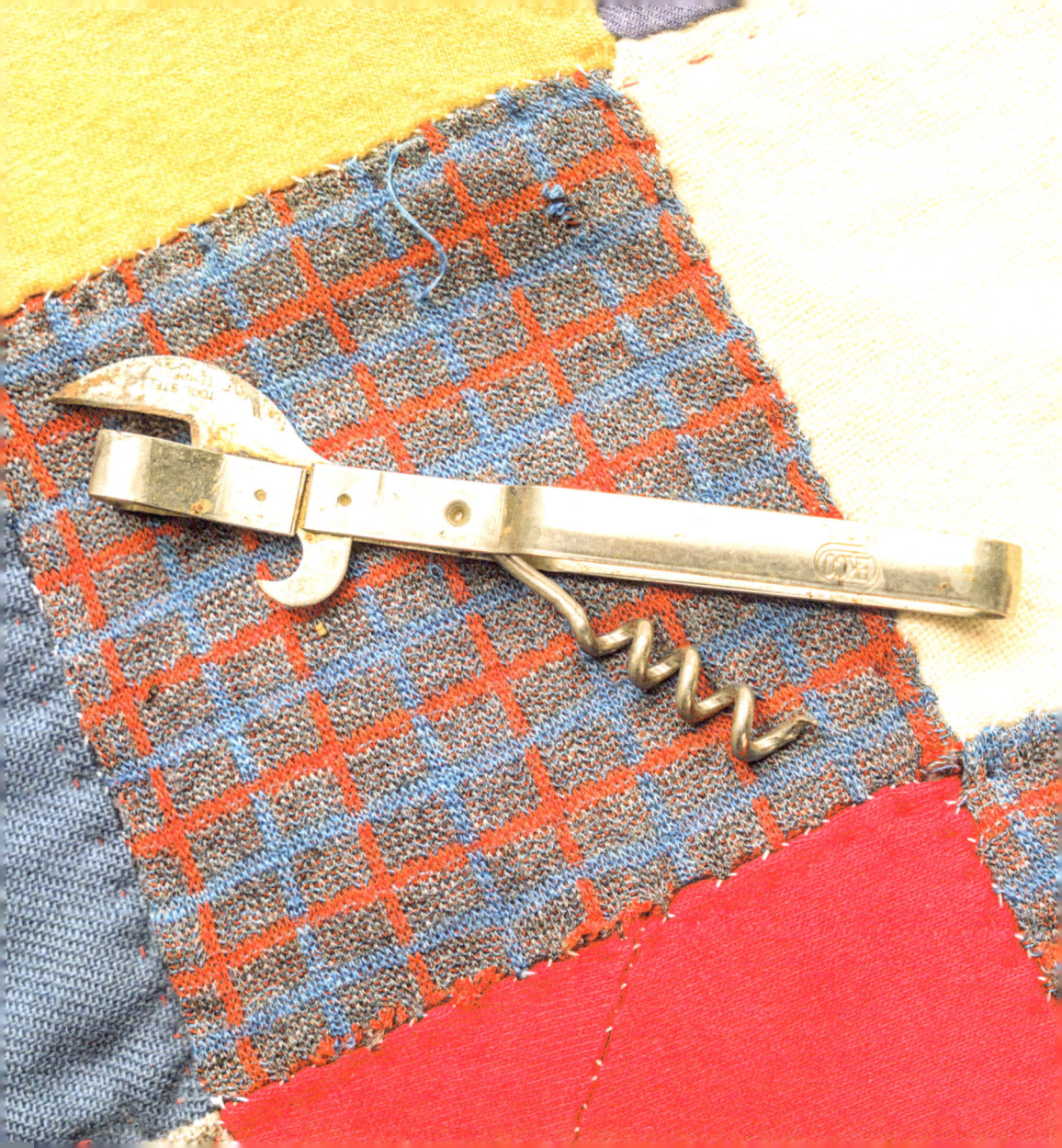

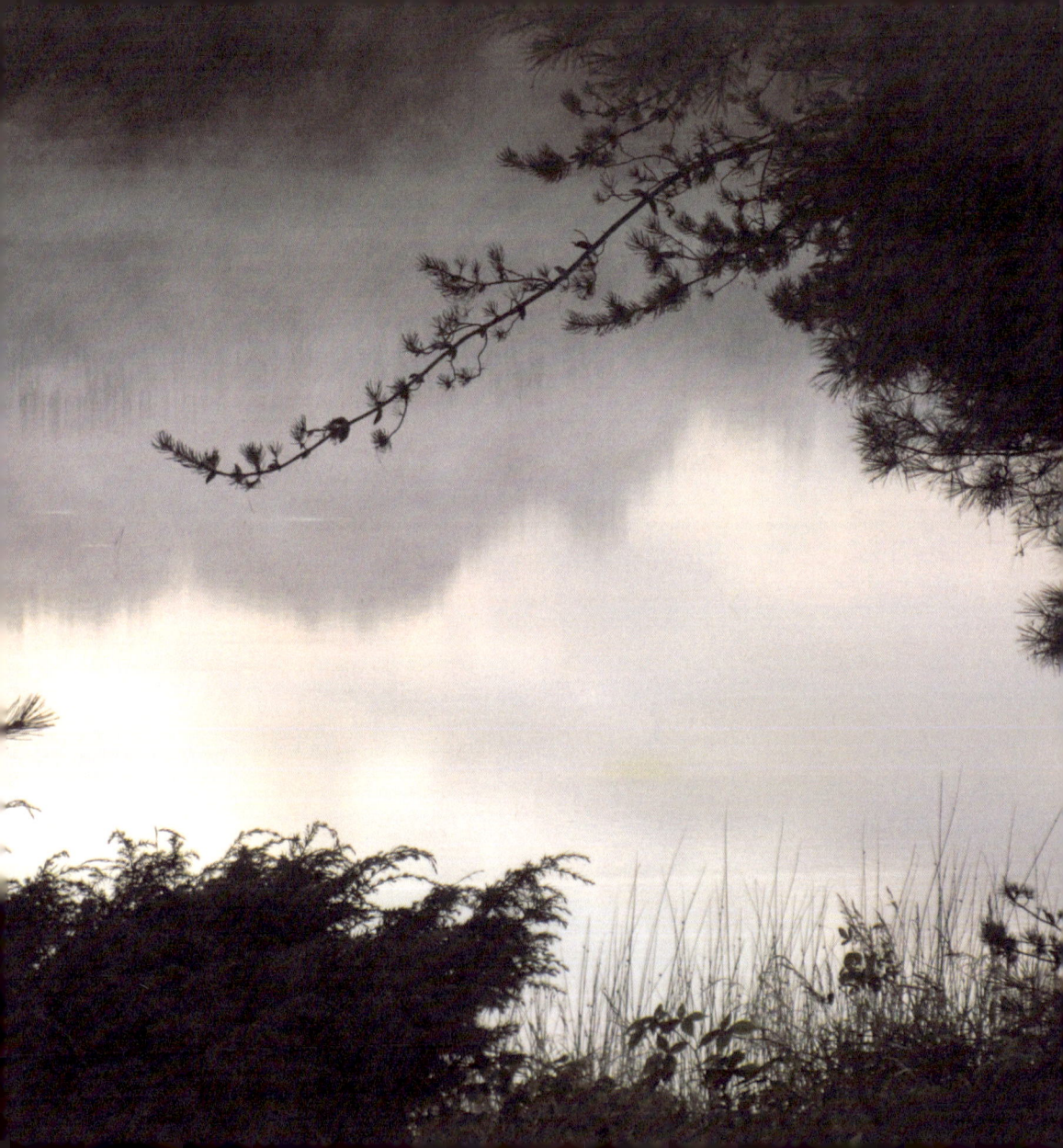

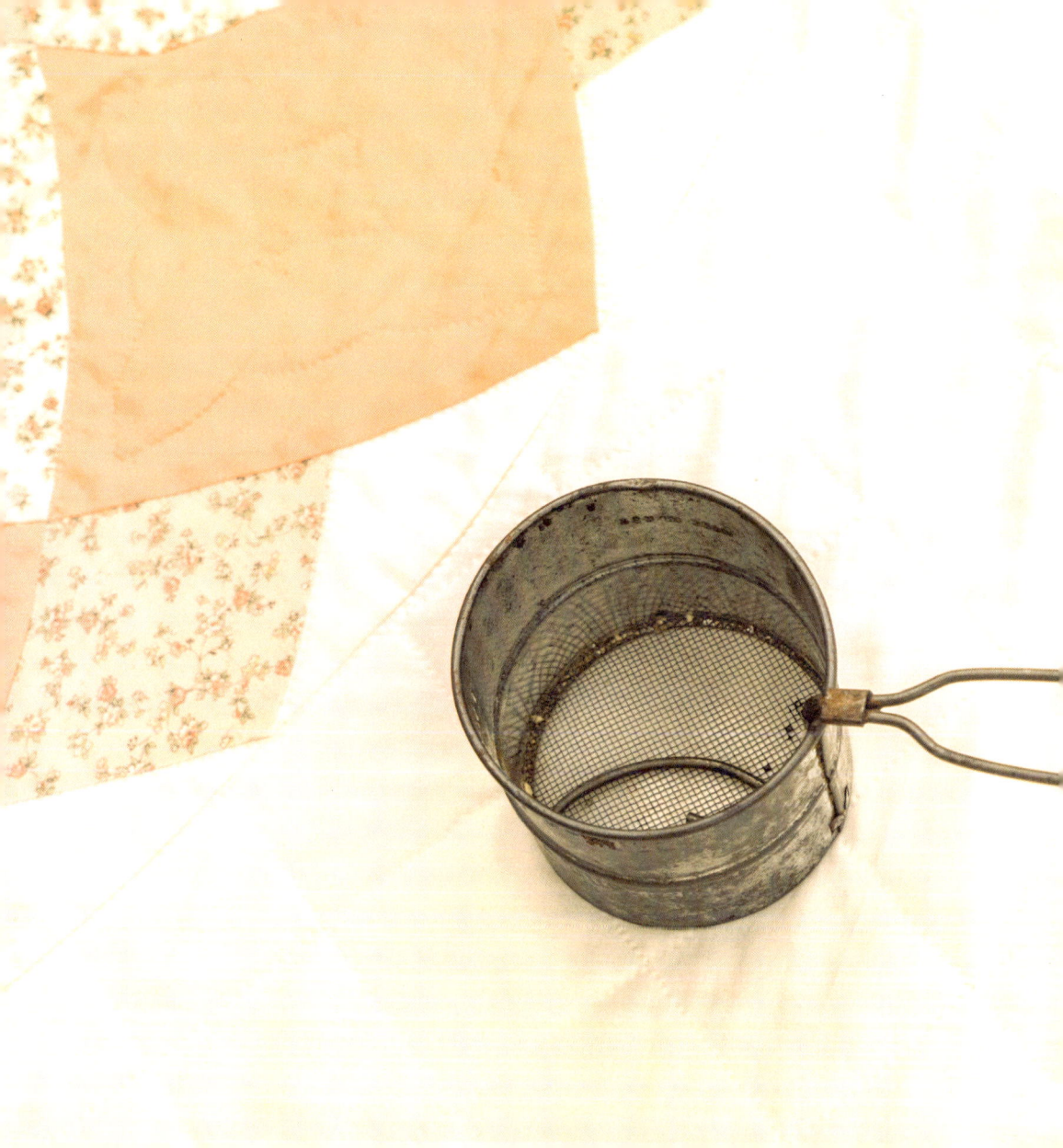

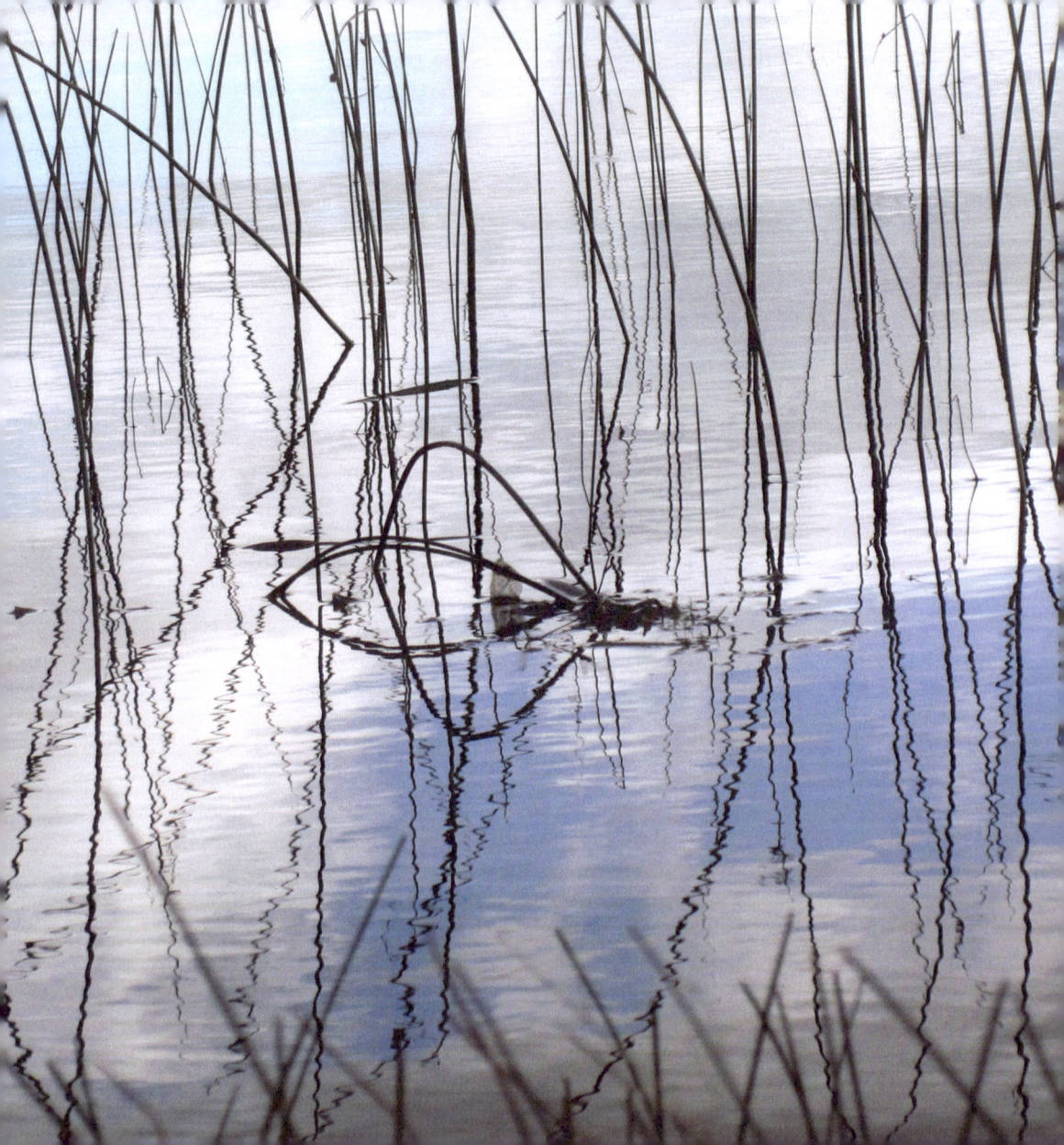

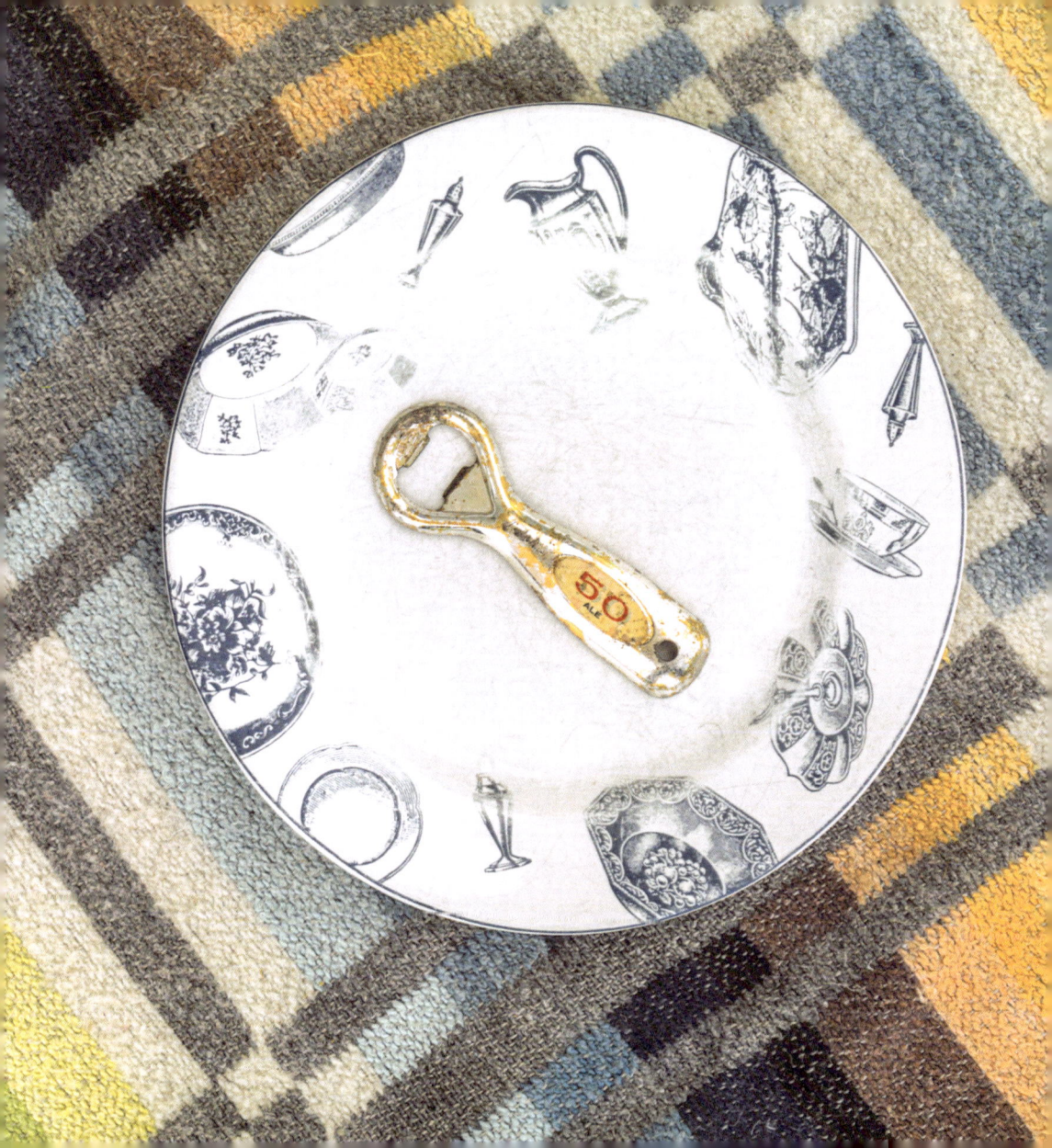

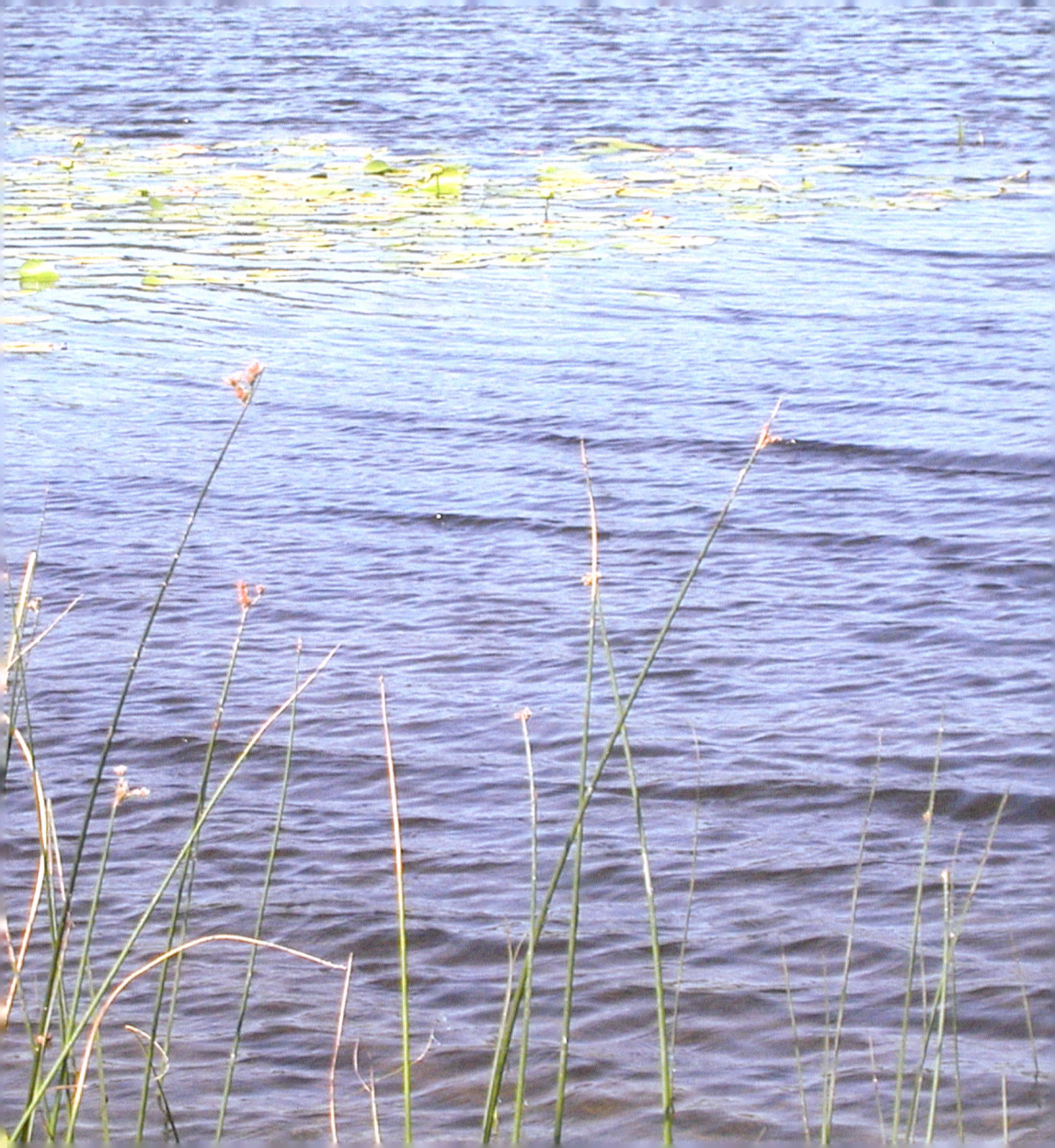

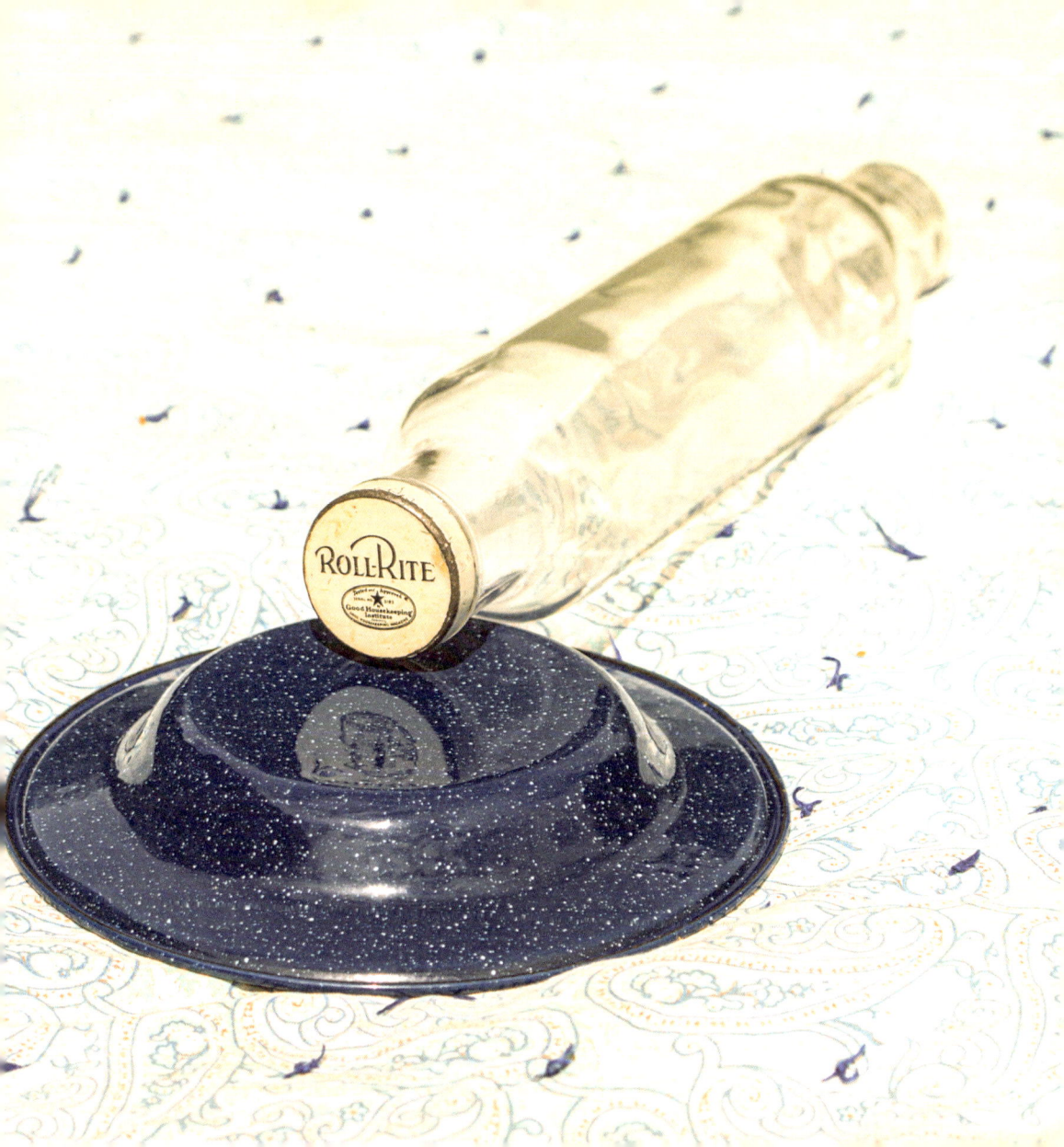

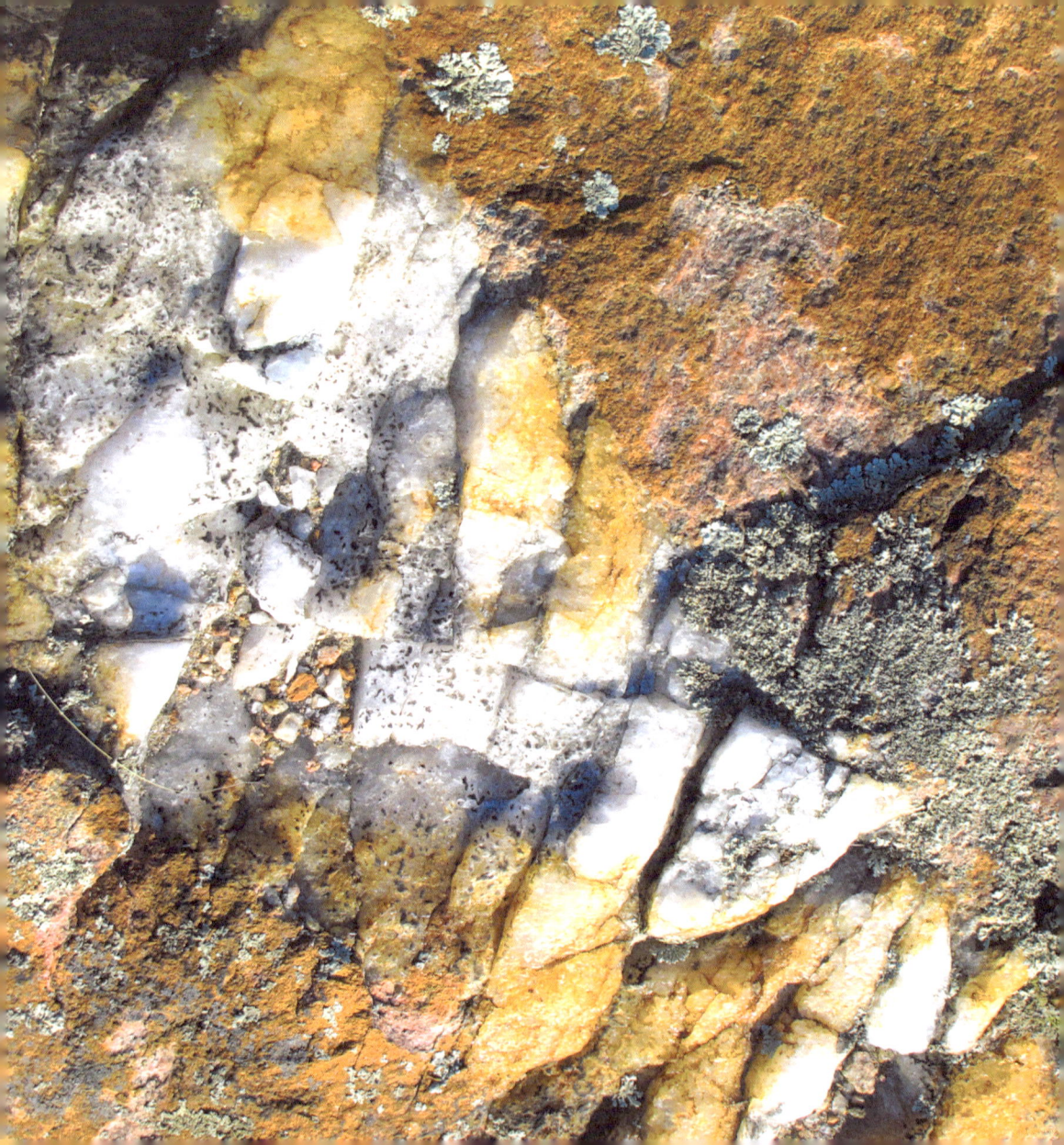

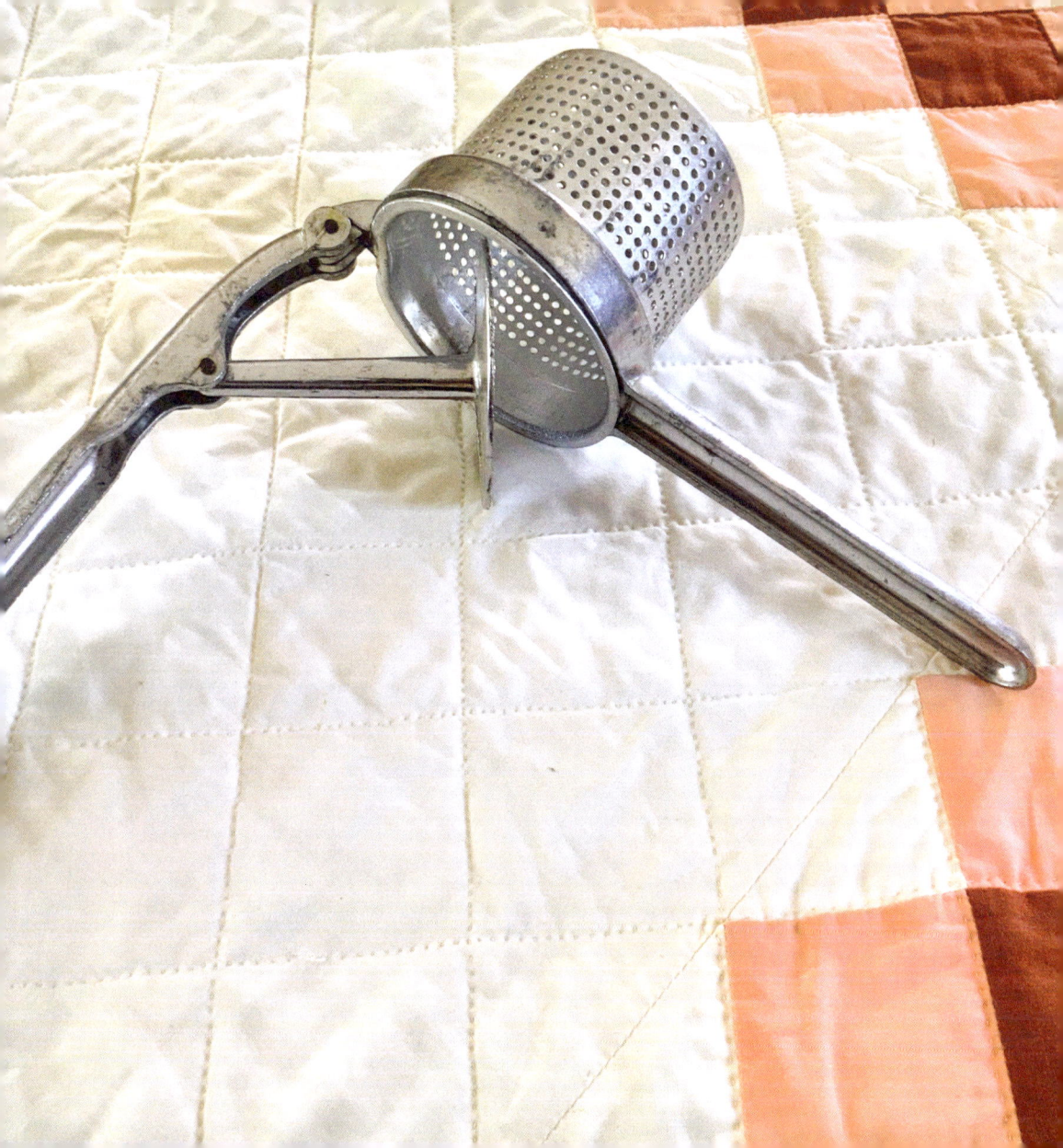

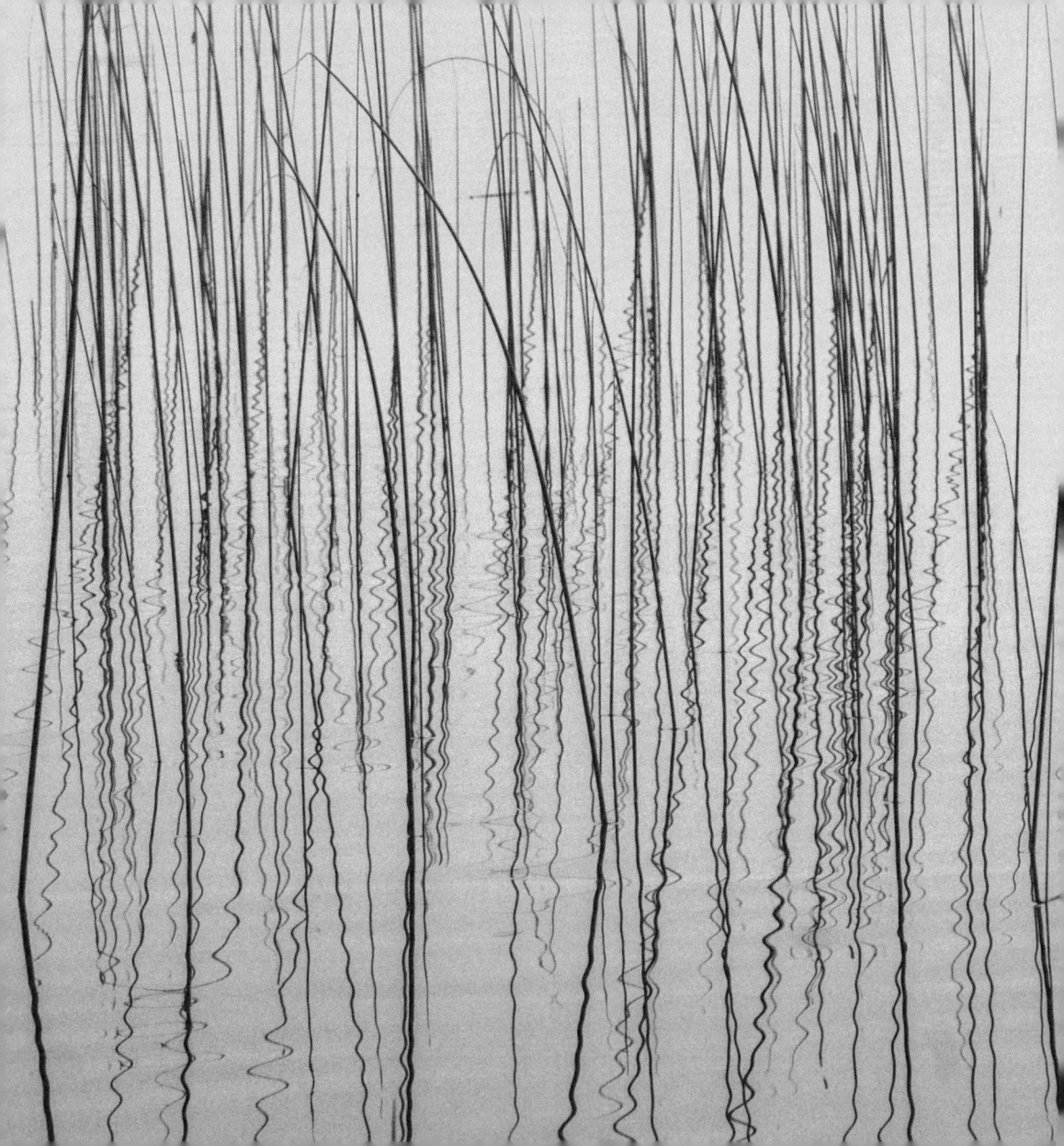

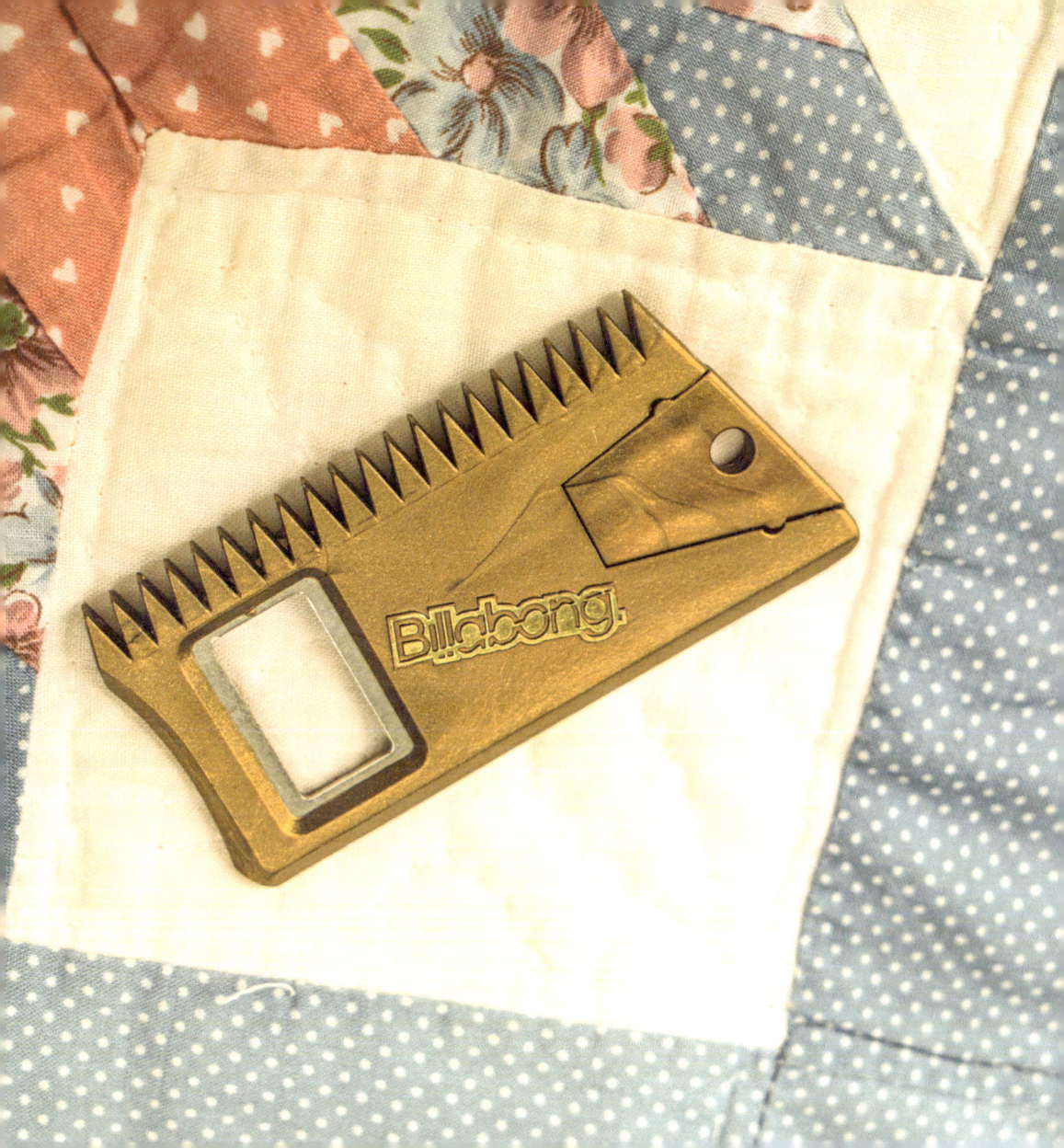

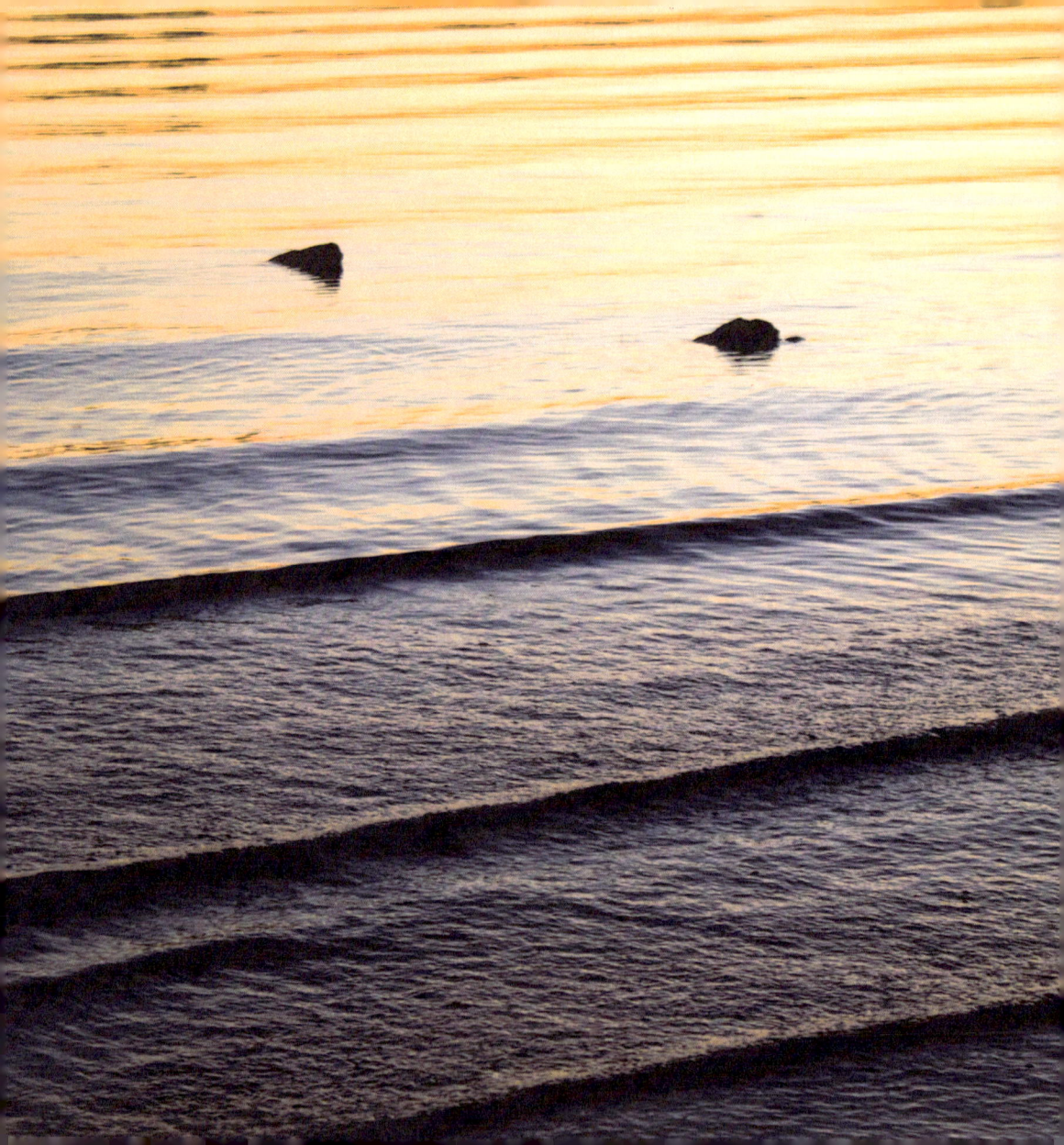

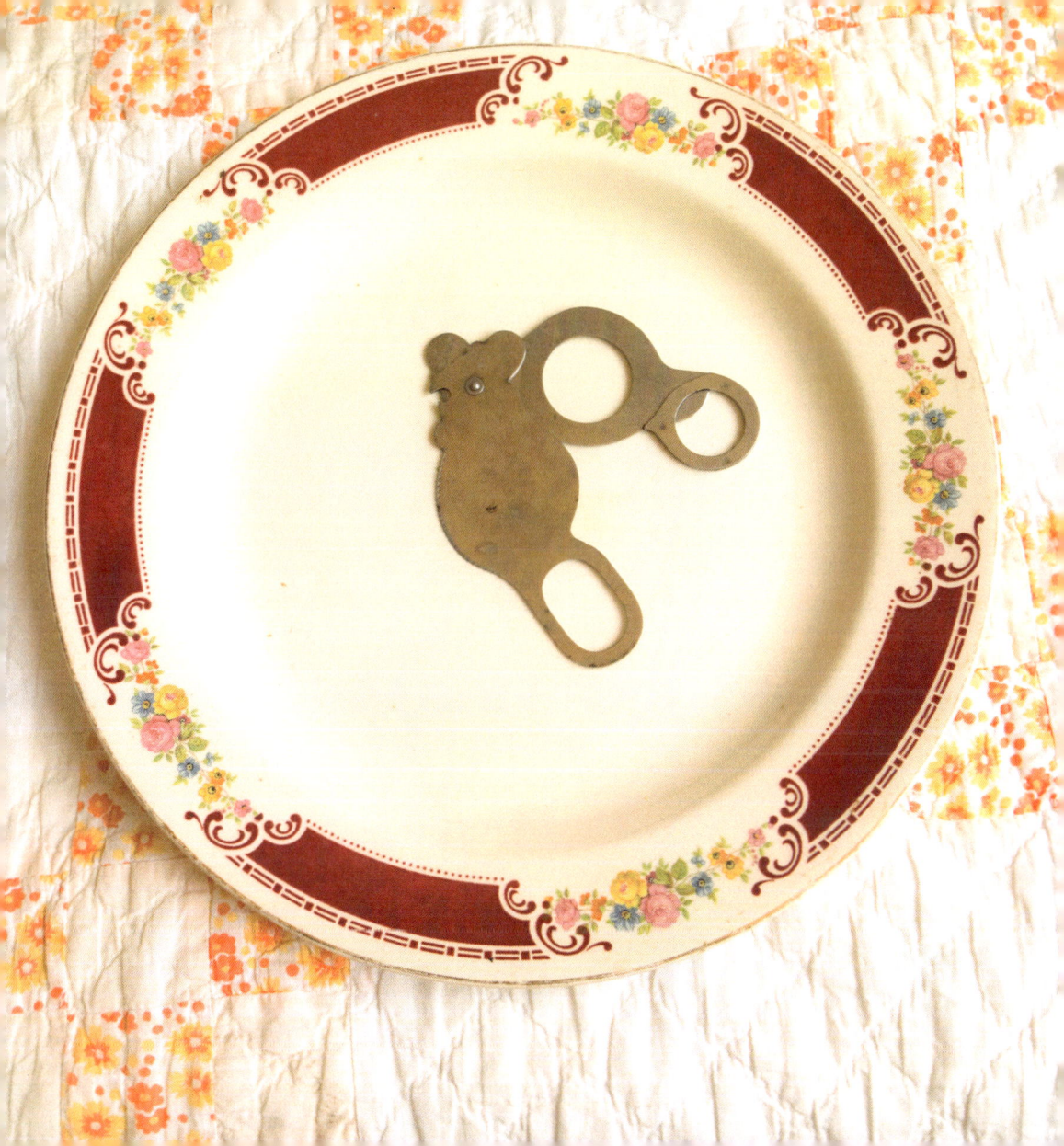

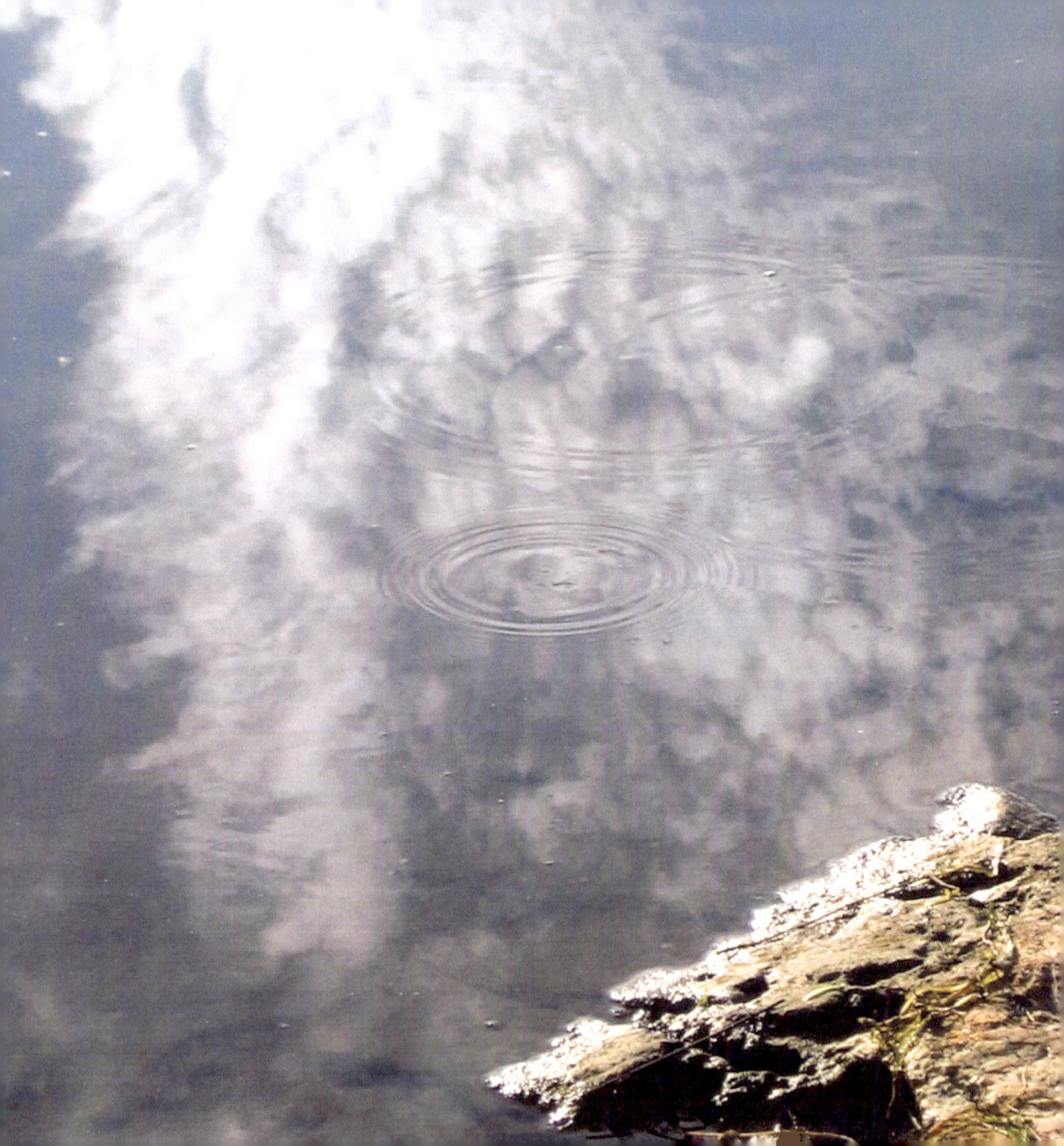

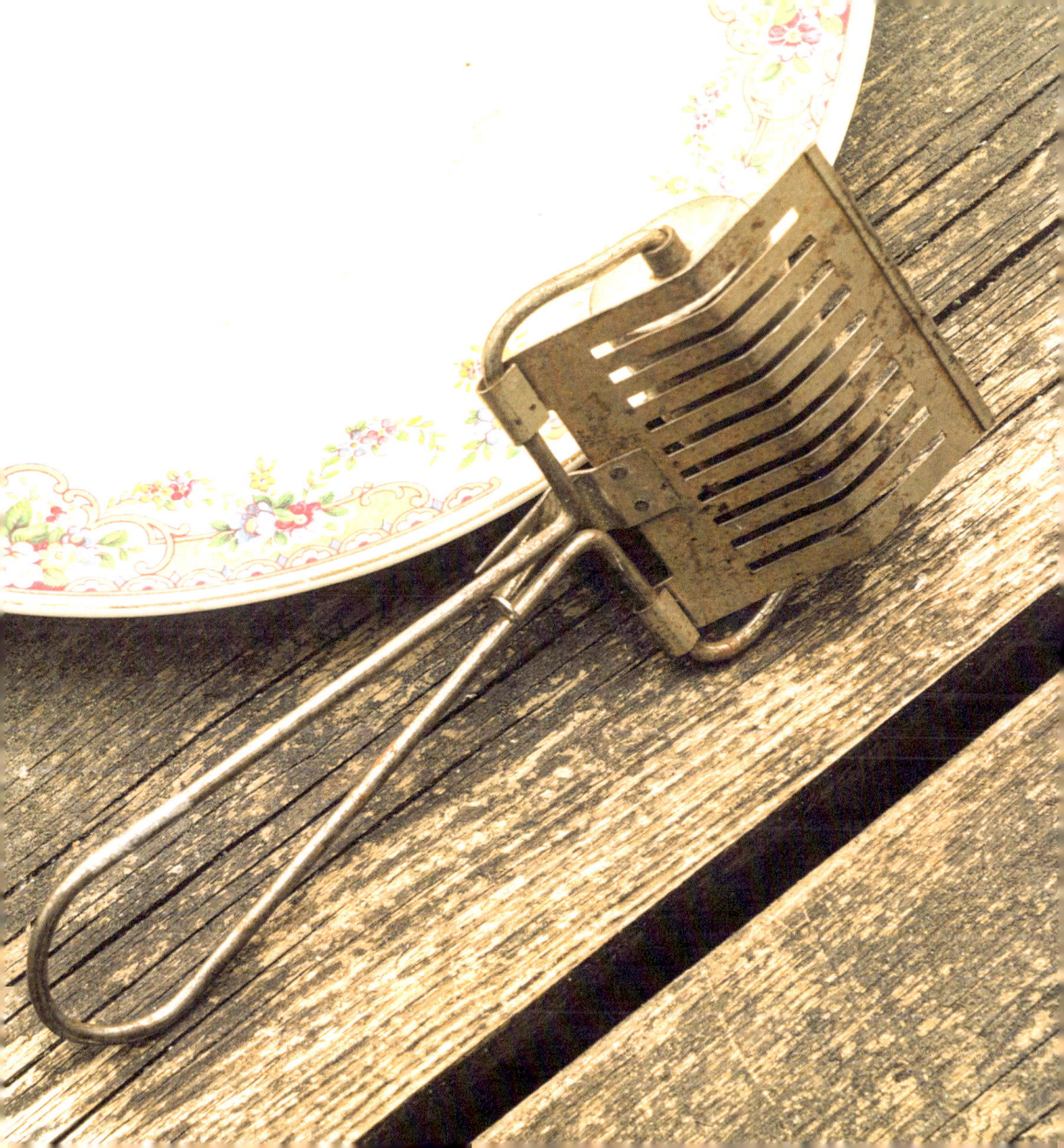

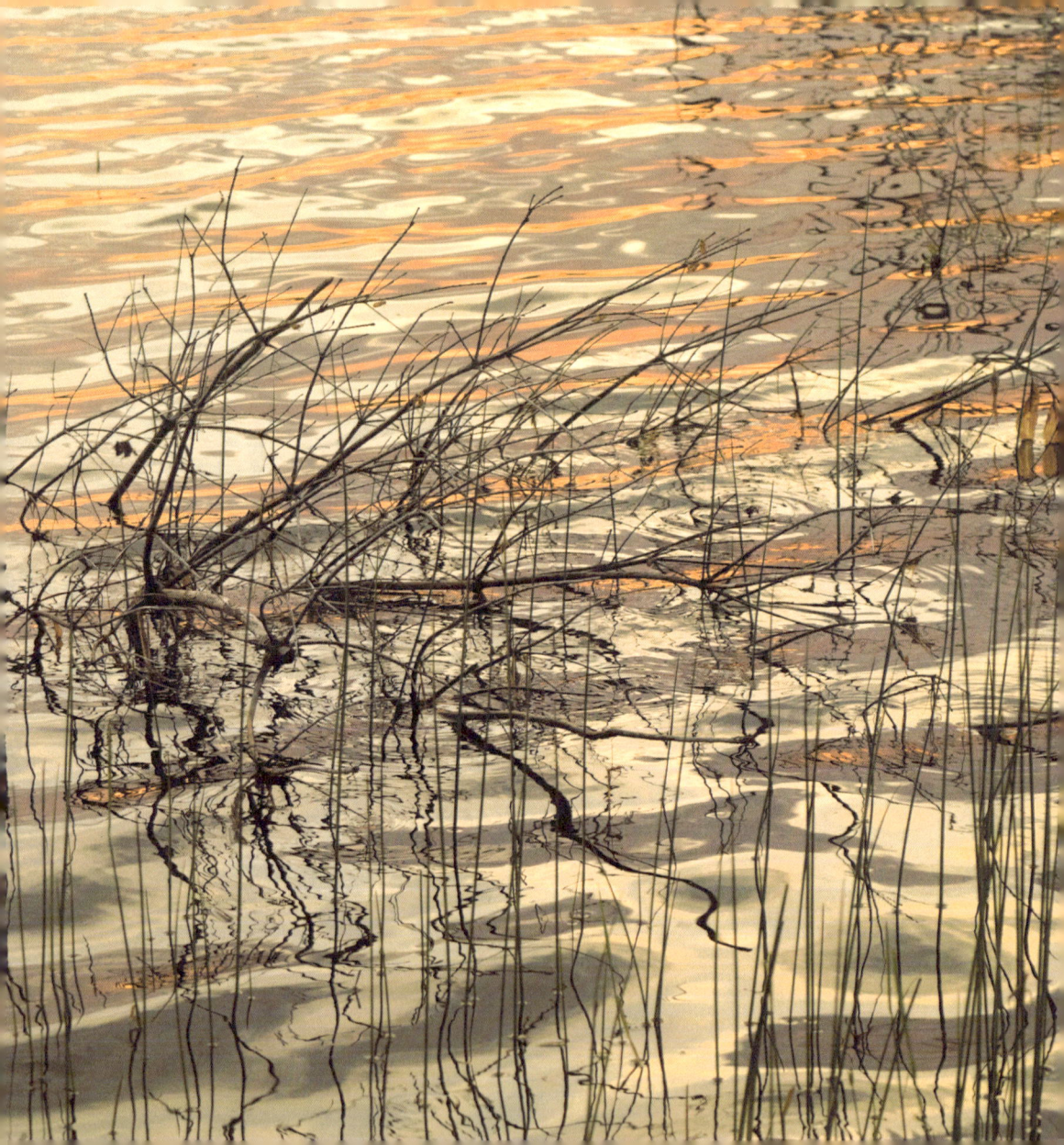

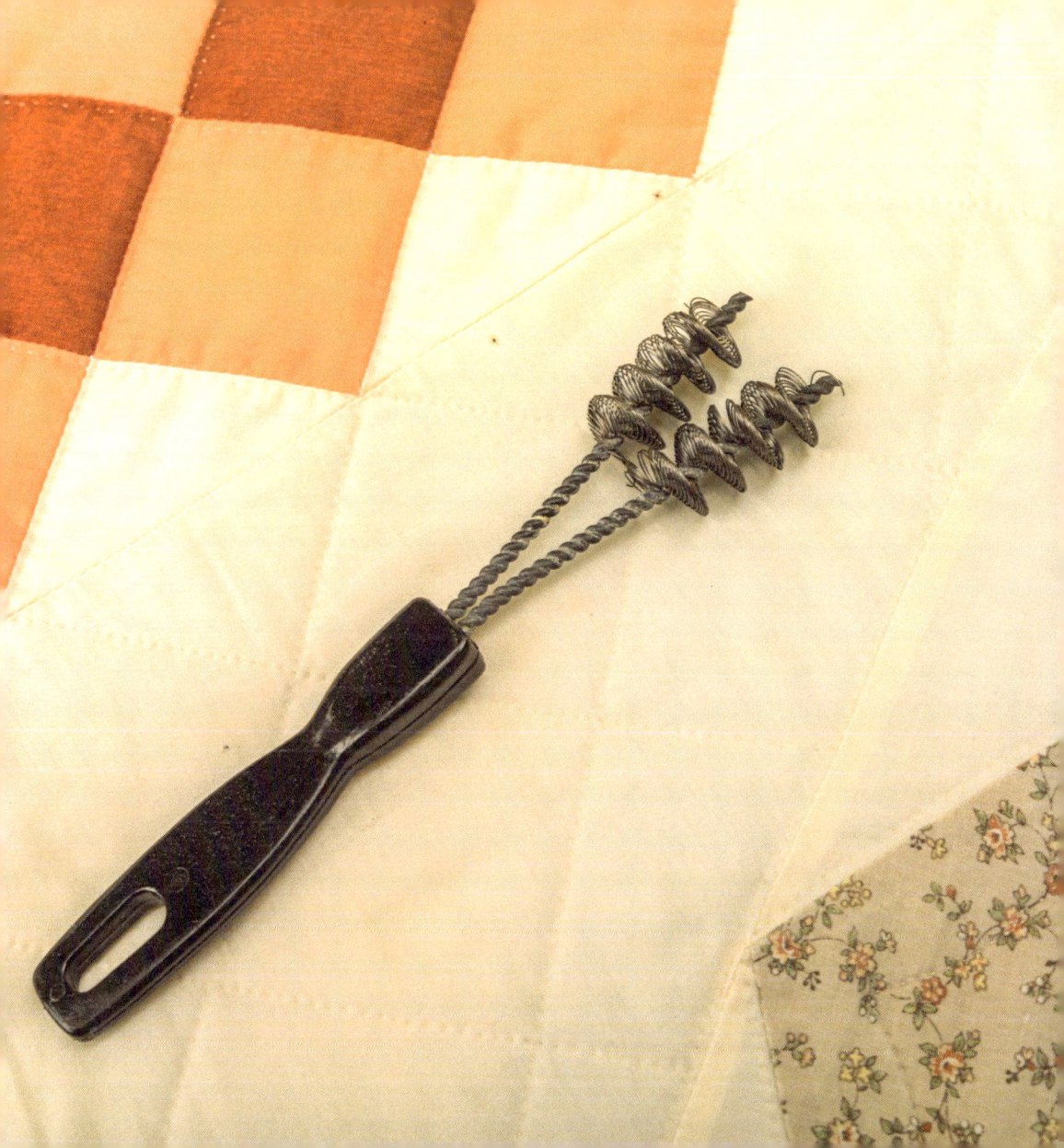

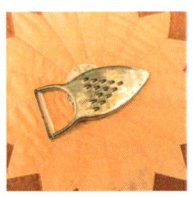

This little grater is so small that it makes me think it's for making lemon zest, and that therefore the vegetable peeler on the tail end is for making longer strips of lemon peel.
Maybe it's a dedicated lemon-gadget!

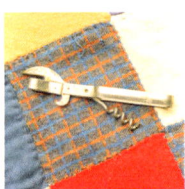

This is a can opener, a corkscrew, and a bottle-cap or lid-opener. Can you imagine how much work it was to open a can using this device?

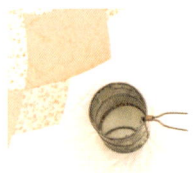

This device is used for sifting flour to get out any lumps, or for sifting flour with baking powder, baking soda, and salt to mix them well. You might still use it!

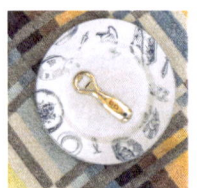

This tool is for opening bottle-caps. Once upon a time, bottle caps did not twist off, and pop-tops for beer cans and soda had not yet been invented. You had to use a bottle-cap opener like this, unless you used your teeth. (That was a guy thing.)

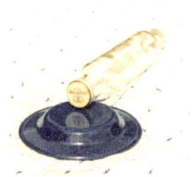

This is a glass rolling pin. It should be filled with ice and water, keeping the bits of butter very cold in the raw pie crust you're rolling out, so that they don't melt into the flour and form a heavy, solid mass. Instead, they will melt only when baked, leaving hundreds of tiny holes--key to a crisp crust!

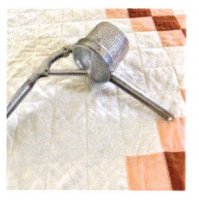

This device is a ricer. It works rather like a giant garlic press. You put into it some peeled, cut-up, boiled potatoes, press it, and the potatoes come out looking like rice. It makes very fluffy "mashed" potatoes.

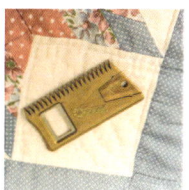

This one's a mystery! The square hole is surely a bottle-cap opener, but what are those teeth for? And what does it have to do with Australia and billabongs?

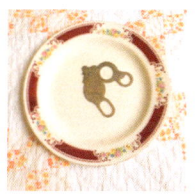

This gadget is highly useful if you are accustomed to eating soft-boiled eggs placed in egg cups. You put the device's hole over the top of the egg, then use the device like a pair of scissors to snip off the protruding eggshell cleanly and neatly.

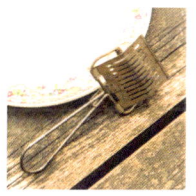

This ingenious but labor-intensive tool is for making fettuccini. Slide the flexible metal shield over your rolled-out pasta dough whilst exerting pressure on the roller by pressing the handle. Roll over the dough, making many strips of raw fettuccini. Repeat many times.

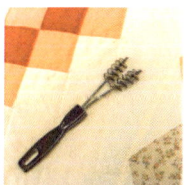

No one has been able to figure this one out. Can you?

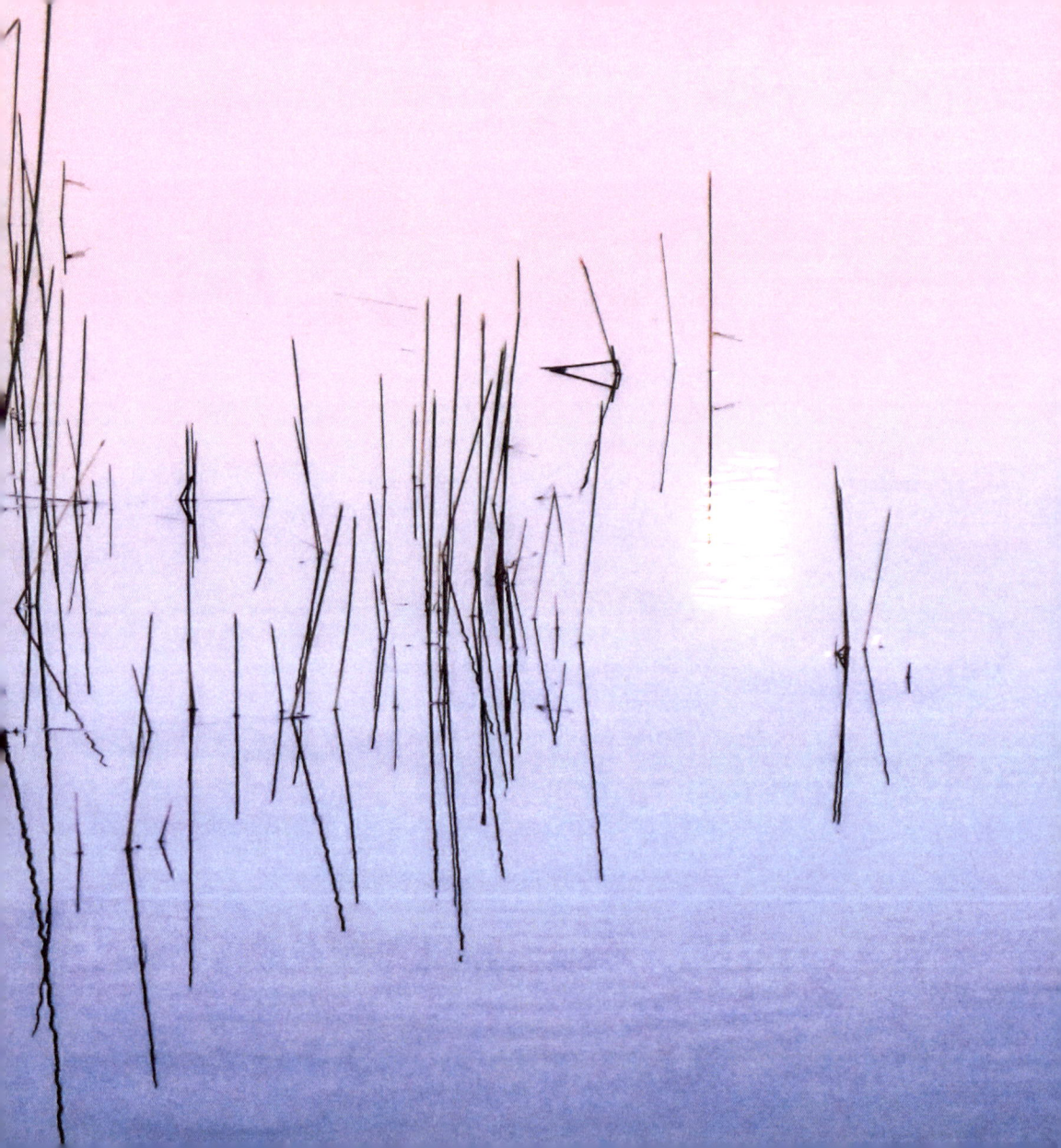

www.ingramcontent.com/pod-product-compliance
Lightning Source LLC
Chambersburg PA
CBRC100912220526
45473CB00010B/2869